Truck Nostalgia

Whitbread Mammoth Major number AE23 was one of the bulk tanker
fleet which carried beer to Brussels bottling plant via BR's
Dover-Dunkerque train ferry in the 1950s.

Truck Nostalgia

Written and photographed
by
Arthur Ingram

BLANDFORD PRESS
POOLE · DORSET

First published in the U.K. 1985 by
Blandford Press Link House, West
Street, Poole, Dorset, BH15 1LL

Copyright© 1985 Arthur Ingram

Distributed in the United States by
Sterling Publishing Co. Inc.,
2 Park Avenue, New York,
N.Y. 10016

British Library Cataloguing
in Publication Data

Ingram, Arthur
    Truck nostalgia.
    1. Trucks—Great Britain—History
    I. Title
    629.2'24'0941   TL230

ISBN 0 7137 1549 9

Typeset by Acorn Origination,
Bournemouth.

Printed and bound in Great
Britain by Biddles Ltd,
Guildford, Surrey.

A Leyland Octopus of Jacob's Biscuits followed by a Mammoth Major of
Bowaters crossing the Holloway Road Archway Tavern junction: see
page 28.

Contents

Introduction

In the following pages an attempt is made, by using contemporary photographs, to depict the road transport scene of the 1950s. The collection is divided into sections, but, as commercial vehicles embrace many manufacturers, models, body types, users, sizes, etc., the sections are to some extent loosely drawn.

I shot the majority of the photographs in the London area, for in those days photography was relatively expensive and my personal transport was limited to a bicycle. However, I arranged a few trips to other parts of the country and a selection of vehicles shot during these is included for variety. Photographic equipment used varied between the ubiquitous Brownie box to a borrowed Leica. As with so many other collections, many of the everyday vehicles were passed over in the continual search for the rare and unusual, and in order to keep costs down it was normal for me to take just one shot of each truck.

Although the main subject matter is the trucks, in most cases all the background on the negative has been included, for they show a wealth of detail of everyday life during the period. One notices how the dress of people has changed over the years – the long 'shorts' of small boys, and the absence of jeans.

While some of the streets are busy with vehicles, others are almost desolate of parked cars, a sure sign of the less affluent times of those early postwar years in Britain. With the vehicles themselves, some have changed little in outward appearance over the years, but other changes make some appear totally antique.

The vehicles of the 1950s were restricted by historic Parliamentary legislation drawn up in the early 1930s and even earlier, but these levels of control pale into insignificance when compared with what was to follow with regard to construction and use, plating and testing, type approval, side guards, tyre laws, noise levels and tachographs.

This was the period when British trucks remained supreme on the home market, and had good export trade as well. These were the days when work and industry seemed to play a more important part in the country, and the heavy lorry was readily accepted as a tool of industry. There was a demand for construction and heavy industry, coal, steel and cement was being exported, and our docks were busy handling ships. The inner cities were alive with industries of all types, and the railways had an enormous fleet of lorries. The British motorway system had yet to be constructed, and much of the country's traffic was on roads completely unsuited to the levels attained by that time, let alone what was predicted in the immediate future.

There was a wide choice of British produced vehicles. For instance, in 1948, some 35 manufacturers of petrol and diesel trucks were offering about 280 different models; by 1953, this had risen to over 350, and the trend was upwards. Electric truck builders totalled about fifteen with around 60 models listed in 1948; this had risen to nearly 90 five years later. This latter category included a lot of small products.

In addition to the fact that many of the old established names, which are no longer with us as individuals, such as AEC, Albion, Morris, Morris Commercial, Trojan, Commer, Karrier, Maudslay, Pagefield, Sentinel and Thornycroft, were still in production, there were also some of the lesser known marques, including Jensen, Proctor, Bradford, Unipower, Vulcan, Standard and Latil.

In addition to all the current makes and types in use, there was also the collection of past products that still abounded, although not all were British. It was possible to come across old Berna, Armstrong Saurer, Renault, Singer, Reliance, Unic, AJS, TSM, FWD, Reo, Mack, Diamond T, Manchester, Willys, Mack, White, Beardmore and others.

So here is a small selection from those days when British lorry production was on the increase. There was a rich choice of individual makes to enjoy; now, it is all part of our past to be seen as truck nostalgia.

Arthur Ingram
London 1984

Delivered to Waring and Gillow before the Great War, this Leyland van ▲ was impressed by the military and sent to France to serve with the British Forces. After the war, it returned home and continued in service until the early 1950s.

Originally supplied to Toft Brothers and Tomlinson in 1938, this model ► DG5/9 passed to HE unit E185, North Derby Group, then to BRS Group 66E and on to become number M7167 of Pickfords, then to Lawrensons after the passing of the 1953 Transport Act.

WARING & GILLOW LTD
WARING & GILLOW LTD
REMOVALS STORAGE SHIPPING
PHONE
MUSEUM 5000.
LONDON, W.1.

LAWRENSONS
LAWRENSONS (Bootle) LTD
MERTON RD
BOOTLE
ERA 963

The Old Timers

Evolution is gradual and can easily slip by without one noticing. Every day trucks get older, and then suddenly they're gone, just as one was thinking 'that's interesting, I must photograph it', or 'I'd like to preserve that'.

When these photographs were taken, the joys of truck preservation were yet to manifest themselves. The days of pilgrimage round breakers yards and showmen's winter quarters, in the search for something interesting, were to follow. These were the days of few enthusiasts, and even then, of the armchair kind. They were also the days of interesting vehicles earning their keep in everyday use, with the drivers and fitters tending them to earn a living.

Some of the vehicles would give today's 'men from the Ministry' a violent nightmare. When the photographs are studied and the equipment noted, it brings home the fact that a driver's life was more difficult than that it is today. But old lorry drivers are made of sterner stuff — none of your wall-to-wall stereo, air conditioned cabs and motorway restaurants for them. No, it was more a case of singing against the noise of the engine, putting on your overcoat and stopping for 'two of toast' at your favourite 'Good Pull Up for Carmen'.

Most of the lorries were petrol engined, and some relied on the cranking handle for starting. The use of anti-freeze was not widespread for commercials, few had semaphore signals, and flashing indicators were unknown. Even adjustable seats were not universal; often the driver sat on a cushion built on top of a box, and a narrow padded backrest separated his spine from the ash framing of the cab.

The variety of trucks which could be seen on the roads of Britain was, of course, far greater than it is today. Even then, there were a few trucks that stood out from the rest because of their age or general appearance. The solid-tyred Dennis shown opposite is one such vehicle, because the vast majority were on pneumatics by this time. These were the days of exposed radiators with their distinctive header tanks and individual nameplates, all in metal or in vitreous enamel.

The 'Old Timers' were almost individuals in themselves as they took on the air of elderly gentlemen, with a leisurely pace and a grandeur all of their own.

These then, are the nostalgia makers.

The Union Cartage employed a sizeable fleet of own-built tractors for ferrying loads of meat carcases from the London docks to Smithfield meat market. By law, it was possible to tow two empty trailers, and in this photograph number 553 pauses at a Silvertown café before entering the docks with its pair.

It is high noon on a sunny day in May 1952 and it appears that the driver of this Islington Borough Council Dennis gully emptier has nipped home for lunch and left a broom under the back wheel 'just in case'. Note the complete absence of parked cars in this North London area of Liverpool Road.

One of the legendary old Leylands operated by United Services Transport for brewers Bass, Ratcliffe & Gretton from the brewery stores near London's St Pancras station, where the casks were transhipped from rail to road after the train journey from Burton-on-Trent in the Midlands.

Bus companies have been notorious for converting buses into lorries over the years, and London Transport have played their part. This London Transport bus shelter lorry is little disguised from its original rôle as a double-deck bus. The low-loading line of the chassis was a definite asset when loading bus shelters from the rear.

Typical of the products of the small volume builders in the 1930s, this little Vulcan Retriever was photographed in Holloway Road in North London in August 1952. Across the busy cobbled road and conduit tramtracks is the showroom of the old Gilford Motor Company which later became a Bedford truck dealership.

Another bus conversion, this time an early AEC Regal in the United Services Transport fleet on the Bass contract. Notice how the very low slung chassis of the old bus has had to be spanned by a chain of cross members to bring the height up to the longitudinal body bearers. It was first registered in 1931 as a coach and lasted as a lorry until the late 1950s.

Typical of the 1930s style of medium range Leyland is this Beaver operated by the Cement Marketing Company. Note the slogan on the headboard which attempts to tell everyone that British cement is the cheapest in the world, although a good advertising man would have painted it larger.

This short wheelbase Leyland Hippo was orginally operated by Hammerton & Co., the brewers, but when sold out of service, the tank was removed for further service. The new owner has fitted a coke-carrying body for his load of general merchandise, hung up his jacket and gone into Bert's Cafe! Note that this hefty machine has to be started by hand, and it should have been fun to drive at night with no nearside mirror and those miniscule headlamps.

There's no doubting that this works ambulance for Willment Bros Ltd was carried on a luxury chassis, but the body does not appear to be in the same category. These were the days when old Rolls-Royces could frequently be seen as ambulances, vans, hearses and breakdown trucks.

Pictured outside the famous Black Cat factory at Mornington Crescent in London is this AEC Monarch box van used for the delivery of Craven A cigarettes. It is doubtful if the period slogan would be acceptable today. Note the autovac on the nearside of the cab, which utilised vacuum created by the engine to draw fuel from the low-slung petrol tank and deliver it to the engine as required.

The twin-steer six wheeler came into prominence in the 1930s in order to achieve a higher payload than a four-wheel lorry without the weight and expense penalty of the traditional six-wheel variety. This 11 ton gross CX27, is a classic example of the type, and was operated by a Smithfield-based meat carrier.

HoVIS
There's
No Gainsaying
You'll
Gain Saying
HoVIS
HOVIS
THE BETTER BALANCED BREAD
HOVIS
26
AXK 6 4

◄ Widely used for long distance freighting by many operators, the six-cylinder Leyland Beaver was designed as a trailer vehicle. Hovis, the flour millers, had several for carrying bagged flour from their Battersea mills to bakers throughout the UK.

► To many truck enthusiasts such things as dustcarts, ice cream vans and the like are much too mundane to deserve a second glance, but they nevertheless have a place in transport history. This tiller-steered Shelvoke & Drewry probably started life as one of the many hundreds of sliding cover type of vehicles which were used by local authorities right through the 1920s, 1930s and 1940s as the mainstay of refuse collection services. When photographed in June 1951, at Poplar, London, quite an ingenious surgical job had been carried out on the body – a Broom & Wade compressor mounted directly on the chassis and an 'air conditioned' crew cab added.

A brilliant sun in the East End of London on a Saturday morning in June 1951 provides the back lighting for this dainty little Thornycroft which was designed for all of 30 cwt! The old established firm of Thornycroft did their best to provide a chassis for every requirement and, during their heyday in the 1930s, listed over 30 models, every one sturdily built to ensure a long lifetime of service. ►

◄For sheer old fashioned obstinacy, this Pagefield deserves a place in this section. Even in 1950, when it was photographed in Hibbert Grove, Lambeth, it was remarkable as a link with the past. Like so many others of its day, it has only one door to the cab, and one assumes that the bonnet side is removed for extra cooling. The military-pattern front tyres were probably obtained at a bargain price, and the absence of any kind of lighting means that it dare not stray too far from home. Although liveried in the name of the Borough of Lambeth, these vehicles – there were quite a number – were operated by F. W. Surridge, who supplied the horsedrawn vans to collect the refuse on the house calls. These were winched up onto the Pagefields when full and taken to a riverside tip for emptying into barges which carried the refuse downstream for discharge on the Thames marshes.

◄Enthusiasts for the AEC marque might well argue that the Y type was as good as the Leyland RAF model any day of the week. Over the years there was always a great rivalry between the two giants in the British heavy vehicle industry although it was more pronounced in the bus fleets up and down the country. This particular Y type was just about at the end of its life when photographed in May 1951 outside the printing works of that late London evening paper *The Star*.

Although Pagefields were used predominantly in refuse collection, some were supplied for haulage purposes. This example was being operated by a Wood Green asphalt contractor when photographed outside the old Palace Gates LNER station in January 1951, originally being in service with J. Lyons & Co., the caterers. ►

Leyland middle weight range of the 1930s was the Cub, which was not built at Leyland but at Ham in Surrey. Both truck and bus chassis were built, in both normal and forward control layout, plus a six-wheeler for longer bodies or special duty. The one pictured is a KG2 model with removal van bodywork seen on a rainy day in Liverpool Road, London. ►

TR
14
THE UNITED AFRICA Co.
LIVERPOOL
FA 1803
lended better

The fact that G. Bailey & Sons Ltd ►
described themselves as 'motor
contractors' is enough to set the
period for this old Manchester tilt
van. The wide open cab, the
absence of headlamps and the
drooping bulb horn all go to
create a period piece in lorry
history, while the style of body
and the 'opening windscreen and
no wiper' just add more
nostalgia.

◄ Although it is widely accepted that
the introduction of the diesel
engine and the blow of taxation
based on unladen weight both
played their part in the demise of
the steam lorry, there were little
pockets of resistance which
continued to keep the steamers
running right through World War
Two and long after. This DG
Sentinel is one of the United
Africa Company's and is seen
running alongside the famous
Liverpool Overhead Railway in the
late 1950s.

Typical of the period pieces which ►
were still in regular use in the
1950s is this Leyland Bull in
service with a Bedfordshire potato
merchant. It was seen on its way
back home from London's old
Covent Garden Market, and the
bemused driver willingly stopped
for a photograph after being
waved down in Seven Sisters
Road!

In the field of vehicle preservation, the name of Ford is well represented, and this is not only due to the fact that there have always been so many of them around. The marque has a great following both in Britain and in the United States, and the Model A along with the legendary Model T is much sought after. The Model AA van pictured above was one old Ford which remained in service until the 1960s and is seen working in the Wembley area of London.

In a bid to speed the Christmas mail, the Post Office hires numerous private vans to swell its not inconsiderable mail fleet. The scene is the old Caledonian Cattle Market near Kings Cross, London, with a model BB Ford of J. Neil and Sons waiting its turn to load.

This immaculate AEC Matador
and Tasker trailer was one of the
splendid selection of vehicles
which took part in the first rally
for old commercials at Beaulieu,
Hampshire, in 1957, prior to the
formation of the HCVC. It had
completed one million miles and
was still in everyday use.

One of the famous Model T Fords
perched forelorn amidst the scrap
of the breaker's yard.
Surprisingly, the tyres seem in
good condition for a scrapper –
who knows, it might have been
preserved!

Back in Civvies

It has often been said that the recent wars have been won by mechanical transport, and that was made clear in World War Two. The vast Lend-Lease scheme whereby the United States supplied huge quantities of equipment for use in the various theatres of war, made Britain's obligation to motor transport very clear.

At the end of hostilities, the surplus vehicles were sold off — much to the delight of people in countries which had suffered the loss of much of their industry, but not of those in countries where the old equipment was in direct competition with struggling postwar factories. The fact that the vehicles were not shipped back to the USA helped to protect the motor industry there.

The huge stockpiles of surplus vehicles went on to the markets in various guises. In some countries, they were used exactly as they stood, complete with soft tops and divisional markings, while at the other end of the scale many were almost completely rebuilt. The rebuilding and adaptation of the ex-military equipment actually helped to create new businesses, with some present day truck builders having started with surplus truck adaptions.

In postwar Britain, the accent was on exports for new vehicles, with restrictions for civilian users. Thus, much of the surplus stock was readily accepted into service with fleets up and down the country. As one would expect, not all the vehicles were suitable for all tasks, although in some cases they were admirably suited, as confirmed by ex-World War Two trucks still in use some 40 years on.

The middle weight trucks, such as Austin, Ford, Bedford and Commer, were absorbed into delivery fleets. Some of the 4×4s were just too high for some work, while others were unduly heavy or expensive on fuel. So many finished their days on site work or as recovery trucks.

The heavier types found use as fuel tankers, heavy haulage tractors and heavy duty recovery units, crane carriers, gritters and snow ploughs. Others were overhauled and exported to start yet another span of life in sunnier climes.

Ford produced a wide range of vehicles for the war effort and the trucks were allocated designations commencing with WOT followed by a model number. An ex-RAF WOTI six-wheeler, when it was in service as a coke lorry from Brentford Gas Works in 1953, is illustrated. It was powered by the legendary V-8 petrol engine, of course.

A fine pair of ex-military machines. The little Morris Commercial 15-cwt tilt truck was used by the gas main maintenance gang, while the model 0854 six-wheel AEC tanker was used for carrying tar from works to tar-sprayers engaged on road surfacing.

Many thousands of wartime Bedfords saw civilian duty long after the war: this OXC tractor unit was one of many operated by the Post Office. The square-nose Bedford was one of the few types of trucks available to civilian operators during the war, although only by way of an MOWT permit.

The K6 Austin was by no means as widespread in the postwar years as the WOT1 Fordson, for whatever reason. This example performed the leisurely duty of a mobile library for the Borough of Hornsey, London, in its later life, a task which suited the long wheelbase chassis.

During the postwar years, the firm of Willment Bros was kept busy on the great rebuilding programmes in London. Pictured here near the famous Barbican in the City is one of their fleet of NR 6×6 Mack tippers, while in the background a QL Bedford does duty as a mobile compressor.

Down in Bermondsey, the Abbey
Garage used this ex-RAF Crossley
Model IGL six-wheeler as its
recovery vehicle. Its specification
included a double drive rear
bogie, Harvey Frost
hand-operated crane and Gruss
air springs at the front.

Ex-military Karriers were less
popular in civilian guise than the
Bedfords and Fords, Austins and
AECs, as least in haulage work.
This six-wheeler employed on
timber haulage has been adapted
with a rather primitive cab.

Long Distance

To many of us, long distance or trunk haulage vehicles represent the peak of the truck world. These are the trucks which attract all the attention and glamour, probably because of their size and the distances they cover. They tend to project an image of superiority over the everyday delivery trucks.

Childhood memories include eight-wheel rigids on 40×8s, articulated Scammells with differing wheel sizes and bouncing along on rubber suspension, the seemingly long lorries and trailers on trunk work, and close-coupled, bow-fronted trailers. The sight of a long line of heavies, the skill of the old-style trunker driver, the atmosphere of the busy night cafe, and the sheer simplicity of the heavy lorry — no frills, no fuss, just functional design for hard work.

Even the painting and lettering designs could imprint the personality of a carrier. Whether it was painted red and gold, blue and white, or green and yellow, the livery and lettering gave substance and quality. 'London and Manchester', 'Long Distance Carrier', 'Daily Service to All Parts' — so went the slogans and messages along the rave or body sides. Some were rather plain, others more fancy, with perhaps a belt round the telephone number, or an artistic monogram but they were never garish.

The drivers' cabs were more angular than those of the 1980s, being mostly of metal panels on an ash frame, providing little luxury for the occupants. But most of the vehicles had their own particular and distinctive shape, with an individual radiator design to enhance the appearance. A headboard was a most regular feature, and it usually concealed the sheetrack on open back vehicles.

Bodywork was mostly the ubiquitous flat or a dropside — just try to find a dropside on a trunk vehicle today! Containers were usually of the old style lift-van type, and then for special traffics such as parcels or the insulated type for meat. Vans were used for parcels, high value goods or those that just had to be kept dry or were too delicate to be roped down. By a wide margin, the most popular was the flat with a substantial sheet and adequately roped.

Everyday scene of the 1950s as a Bedford OY Luton van of Amalgamated Removers and Transport Ltd of St Albans crosses the Thames in view of Windsor Castle on the old road to Slough. Period features in the photograph include the Matchless motorcycle, Wolseley and Austin cars, single white line and the complete absence of TV aerials and double yellow lines!

A late evening shot of a Kentish Town depot BRS Scammell as it emerges from the railway bridge at the bottom of Barnet Hill, London, and heads into the setting sun on its way north. This section of the old Great North Road was useful for getting photographs in the fading light of evening because there were no buildings to create shadows and the vehicles were going at a moderate speed.

A clutch of BRS eight-wheel trunkers parked at Whetstone by the shunters, await the arrival of the long distance night trunk drivers. The Scammell on the left is based at Greenheys depot in Manchester, while the Bristol, specially designed for BRS trunk work is from the parcels depot at Rushden, Northants. The Leyland Octopus is based at Blackwall Tunnel depot in London.

A rather quiet scene at the Archway Tavern junction at the top of Holloway Road, as a Liverpool-based Leyland Octopus of Jacob's Biscuits leads an old taxicab and a Mammoth Major of Bowaters across the famous junction. For very many years, this area of north London witnessed a never ending stream of heavy trucks both in and out of the capital.

Pictured outside the parcels depot at Goswell Road is a postwar Leyland Beaver and trailer which has brought a load from Nottingham. The brilliant early morning sun highlights one of the safety chains which connects vehicle and trailer, while one of the locals pauses to admire the advertisement on the body side.

Soon after the Transport Act 1953 was passed and the sale of sections of British Road Services was finalised, the long distance fleets took on a new look. W. H. Bowker of Blackburn was one of the companies which re-entered haulage, their earlier fleet having been acquired by the Road Haulage Executive following the passing of the Transport Act 1947. Here, in the early evening, vehicles are being prepared for the long night trunk northwards.

Loaded and rolling – old style. An old Leyland Beaver and trailer swings onto the North Circular Road at Stonebridge Park in 1955. Looking rather down-in-the-middle, vehicles of this type gave yeoman service for very many years. The fact that the front wheels of the trailer have no mudguards is typical of the type, but the lorry should have them on the rear.

Not all long distance traffic was carried by the maximum capacity eight-wheelers. The ubiquitous four-wheeler was often the mainstay of fleets whose traffic did not demand anything heavier. This was also the heyday of that fast disappearing phenomenon: the tramper. He might be away from home all week taking loads from A to B to C and so on — tramping round the country.

Even after nationalisation, when all the BRS lorries were painted plain red and all the vans green, it was still possible in many cases to distinguish the original owners. This fine example of a six-wheel rigid Scammell has the cross boarded timber body which was typical of Eastern Roadways.

Typical of Albion design in the 1950s is this articulated outfit of E. Wells & Son of Rotherhithe, bonded carriers. The semi-trailer has the unusual four-in-line wheel arrangement, and, for greater stability when uncoupled from the tractor, it has fold-down legs to support the front of the trailer.

Scottish vehicles have long been renowned for their fine paintwork and good turnout. Pictured here are a pair of AEC Mammoth Majors which have journeyed south and wait their turn to unload in a quiet London street. Nearest the camera is the later version of the Mark III with the metal front, which replaced the type with the exposed radiator, second in this picture.

One of Fisher Renwicks showboat Scammells pictured soon after its first coat of nationalised green, and showing the early system of BRS lettering before the group system was adopted. These large vans were the highest trunk vehicles operated and were soon to be cut down to something more manageable following innumerable accidents in the hands of inexperienced drivers.

The shape of long distance trucking — late 1950s style. A bright silver AEC Mammoth Major operated by the Tate and Lyle subsidiary Silver Roadways, leads a Scammell of Buckleys of Warrington up the old Great North Road at South Mimms. Note that this late model Mark III, with the 'tin front' style cab, still retains the opening windscreen.

A scene not to be repeated: an Albion CX eight-wheeler of Valley Carriers, Penarth, leaves the famous Tower Bridge over the River Thames, when it was one of the major transport crossings. Being the last bridge before the mouth of the river, and close to both the London and the Surrey Docks, meant that this Thames bridge was the busiest.

G. L. Baker is an old established haulage company which returned to operations after the 1953 Transport Act was put into effect. A mixed fleet of Bedford, Albion, Dennis, Leyland, ERF and Rutland vehicles made up the operation, with headquarters at Stratford, in east London. The vehicle in the photograph heading north on the night trunk was a Rutland conversion of an older AEC chassis.

Tartan Arrow Service was set up in the late 1950s to handle parcels traffic between London and Glasgow, using a fleet of box vans of which this Scammell 8×2 is an example. Also included in the fleet was an unusual AEC Reliance bus chassis with box van body. Later on, the company switched to using their own particular design of containers and transferred to rail for the trunk haul, even going as far as having their own road/rail transfer depots.

Richardson (Hull) Transport Co., were the operators of this postwar Maudslay Mogul, pictured as it pulls away on the night trunk along the old A1 road at Finchley. Note the old style van trailer, which is carried on single wheels all round and has security chains should the towing eye or towbar come adrift.

During the postwar years, the Jensen light weight six-tonner was quite a popular machine for bulky traffics. It was produced as a dropside, or as a capacious Luton van as shown here, and was of light metal construction for a minimal unladen weight and low vehicle taxation. The design was originated in the 1930s by Jensen Motors in collaboration with Reynolds Tubes for the transport of long lengths of tubing used in the aircraft industry.

In Britain, the use of drawbar tankers is limited to those carrying non-hazardous loads such as margarine, milk, tar and foodstuffs. The only place where fuel tanker combinations are seen is within the confines of airports. The AEC and trailer seen here was part of the fleet of Harold Wood & Sons Ltd, who quickly built up a large business of tank haulage in the late 1950s.

A.R. MARSHALL & SONS LTD
LAU 6

Typical trunk vehicle of the 1950s pictured after loading newsprint at Liverpool. The use of rigid eight-wheelers in Britain dates from the late 1920s when Sentinel introduced their steam wagon with four axles. Petrol and diesel-powered versions followed soon after, with AEC, Leyland, Foden, ERF and Atkinson models being offered.

Fine example of the AEC Mammoth Major Mark II rigid eight, widely used for trunk operations, as a flat for general haulage or, as in this instance, a high capacity box van for woollen goods. This BRS-owned example is pictured heading out of London on the old A1 road at Highgate, Middlesex. Period features include the following traffic which includes one of the popular Austin '3-way' vans, and the Westminster Bank in the days before joining with the National Provincial.

The majority of BRS trucks were plainly painted with very little lettering, usually just the operating group name and a fleet number, plus of course the 'hungry lion' on the doors. This Atkinson of Coventry depot in the Midland Division of BRS was one of the few variants, fitted as it is with the 'Coventry to London, Express Nightly Service' headboard.

The name of Chivers has been linked with that of vehicle preservation for very many years because the RAF-type Leyland owned by the Historic Commercial Vehicle Society is still maintained in the Chivers livery. It was presented to the former HCVC very many years ago. The L1586 Atkinson shown is equally well turned out, and was typical of the fleet used to distribute the famous preserves around the country.

The mainstay of the postwar Commer range was the well-proven Superpoise models in the two to five-ton payload size. The all-new forward control QX range was added in 1948, and first appeared with the underfloor petrol engine. This was followed by the introduction of a diesel-engined version in 1954 featuring the revolutionary TS 3 two-stroke, which embodied the opposed piston layout, having just three cylinders but six pistons. A six-wheel version was introduced later, as shown, which had a Unipower rear bogie.

The 12-ton payload Jubilant was the top of the range produced by Dennis for many years, for, although eight-wheel chassis were built, production was limited to a handful. Ritsons of Liverpool operated this insulated container lorry for the transport of frozen meat carcasses for Towers Meats on journeys from meat markets.

John Buckley of Warrington had a fine fleet of both rigid and articulated Atkinsons in the 1950s, each carrying a fleet name. In the photograph we see *Thunderbolt* heading out of London on a night trunk. Note the old style of wooden dropside body with hoops and tilt, a feature not seen on eight-wheelers today. Curtain sided bodies and the TIR style of tilt cover have largely replaced the old tilt designs of years ago.

A long line of mixed traffic headed by a Mark II Mammoth Major creeps gingerly down the Archway Road in London beneath the famous bridge after a snowstorm in January 1955. This road was the main route to the north and north-west before the M1 was opened, and was an ideal spot to study the trunk vehicles of the day.

In common with other manufacturers in the 1950s, Seddon of Oldham were adding to their product range. The very popular 6-tonner was supported from below by the Mk 7 3-ton chassis plus the intriguing little normal control 25-cwt with Perkins three-cylinder diesel engine. The Mark 14 illustrated was one of the larger models produced at the time, being a 24-ton chassis with Gardner 6LW engine. Notice the lightweight design of semi-trailer with latticework type of mainframe.

During the 1950s, it was unusual to see foreign trucks in Britain, for the cross channel roll-on/roll-off ferries were in their infancy, except for the old established railway ferries. Sutton & Son of St Helens were among the first handful of hauliers to handle European trailers, having an arrangement with a Belgian haulier, L. Van Gaever of Antwerp, whereby loaded trailers were collected from the ferry terminal and the loads distributed without transhipping.

An unusual style of Commer long wheelbase lorry and trailer, with special jigs for the transport of Humber car body shells from the Acton factory of British Light Steel Pressings to the assembly plant at Coventry. The outfit has the style of cab usually fitted to Karrier chassis, and could probably have been specified by the Rootes Group in the interests of economy. It was operated by British Road Services from their Perivale contracts depot.

One of the attractions of the Commercial Motor Show at London's Earls Court was the practice of displaying vehicles in operators' colours instead of the overall plain colours presently adopted by vehicle manufacturers for their exhibition fleets. Equally attractive was the provision of vehicle displays outside the main exhibition building.

The ERF eight-wheeler was a popular chassis among long distance carriers. This pre-war example was among the fleet operated by P. A. Carter & Sons, who were one of the first free enterprise hauliers to recommence operations after denationalisation in 1953.

This Maudslay Meritor of BRS Bradford Parcels group is about to set off on its night run to Yorkshire. Many of the trunk vehicles employed on the parcels service ran with box van drawbar trailers, but on this occasion a load of transformers on a flat trailer make up the outfit. Note the substantial front bumper, positioned at loading bank height to prevent damage to the cast aluminium radiator.

Solebay Street, London E.1, and the surrounding streets were the scene of much activity in the 1950s. For this was the London operating base of Davis Bros (Haulage) Ltd, who operated a large fleet of tankers, vans and flats to all parts of the country. This Leyland Octopus was one of many tankers on hire to Charringtons for the distribution of Mobil fuel oil.

Heading north into the setting sun goes one of the handful of Thames Trader six-wheelers of J. G. Fielder of Bradford. The unusual overcab body extension with support irons down to the front of the chassis members enables a large load of wool to be carried.

Pictured in Kentish Town at the end of its working life with BRS, is one of the ex-General Roadways Scammells. With its bow fronted semi-trailer carried on large section single tyres, it is typical of the trunk vehicle of pre-war days.

In the early postwar years hordes of car delivery drivers, each clutching his set of trade plates, delivered most new cars from factory to showrooms round the country. The double-deck car carrier started a trend which continues unabated, as designers produce models with greater capacity. This underfloor engine Commer shows the state of the art in the 1950s, when five or six cars was the normal load. The extensive under-bumper silencer system is the Rootes two-stroke diesel's hallmark.

It could fairly be said that this Atkinson drawbar outfit of Sutton & Son (St Helens) Ltd marks the epitome of British trunk haulage in its day. The Sutton vehicles are always well turned out, and the loads adequately sheeted and roped. This photograph was taken when trailers required a trailer attendant, and many operators were switching to articulated trucks in order to carry a maximum legal load with just a driver.

Swinging round the Tally Ho!, North Finchley, one-way system, on its way north during the evening, goes the attractive Leyland Steer and drawbar trailer of Harrisons of Dewsbury. The Luton van body has a sheet over the roof loading hatch, and the trailer has a fitted sheet to protect the woollen goods.

Nylon was a comparatively new material in the 1950s, and its applications were few compared with today. In the livery of British Nylon Spinners, and owned by H. Pye and Sons, this Atkinson M1266 with integral cab and body was of a type which was not all that common when it was new and the practice of building special cab and door panels to match van bodywork was rare outside furniture vans.

The Meat Cartage Service of BRS acquired a large fleet from such operators as Pickfords, Hayes Wharf, Matthews, Fairclough, Dawsons and Routh & Stevens. This Maudslay Mogul ballast box tractor was originally in service with T. M. Fairclough as a crane lorry for the handling of church bells from the Whitechapel Foundry.

A familiar sight after the passing of the 1953 Act, which broke up the BRS monopoly of long distance road transport, was the piggybacking of vehicles back to base for overhaul before entering regular service. This scene was photographed at Camden Road, north London, in October 1954.

Since 1934, ERF of Sandbach, who pride themselves as being Britain's last remaining independent truck builder, have produced a fine range of 'oil engined lorries', as their advertisements used to say. Shown here is one of the large fleet of ERFs operated by Union Cold Storage on meat transport between dockside, market and warehouses and stores throughout the country.

A cement-covered road highlights a Mark III Mammoth Major of BRS Stoke branch, as it waits at a cement works to be loaded with flints destined for the glazing of Potteries earthenware.

Waiting quietly under the arches of Kentish Town depot for the arrival of the night trunk driver to take over, is this British Road Services Atkinson eight-wheeler. This London yard was previously the premises used by General Roadways Ltd, and had remained the terminal for much of the general haulage traffic to and from the north-west of England.

Most trucks which form the medium weight range are of the two-axle type, while the three-axle variety, being that much heavier, is usually for tipper or mixer applications. The Commer Superpoise illustrated here is a somewhat rare type to be seen in general haulage, even though the long body space must have made it attractive. Drawbacks of the design include a high unladen weight, a heavy fuel consumption with a petrol engine and a heavy handful for the driver with no power steering.

This BRS Bristol eight-wheeler is numbered in the fleet of Exeter depot, but lettered for the road transport clearing house Co-ordinated Traffic Services. With branches at London, Liverpool and many towns and cities in the south-west, Co-ordinated were among the largest of clearing houses who act as the market place between suppliers and users of road transport. The vehicle is parked outside the BRS 9A depot, which handled mostly contract hire vehicles.

The Seddon DD8 was the culmination of many years of experience in the sphere of lorry building by Seddon Diesel Vehicles of Oldham. Their early diesel-engined 6-tonner had earned a considerable reputation as a simple, no-frills goods vehicle, using trusted components such as Perkins engine, Kirkstall axles and David Brown gearbox. The example illustrated was the first of its type, being employed on long distance work by the Cyprien Fox Group.

The best remembered epitaph for the giant British Road Services operation of the early 1950s is undoubtedly the Bristol range of heavy trucks, which marked the entry of the nationalised concern into vehicle building. The first model, the HG6L rigid eight-wheel chassis was not quite all-Bristol though, for it included a Leyland engine. The vehicle shown above was based at the Brentford depot and is shown with a palletised load of Heinz canned food loaded at their Willesden factory in north London.

Tankers and Bulkers

Truck operators have always striven to load their vehicles to capacity, for obvious reasons, and the advantages of moving a large batch of any commodity in one container is uppermost in the mind of the traffic manager. If it can be 'bulked' instead of packaged in small lots, it just has to be cheaper to transport.

So, on looking back through truck history, we find that there were tankers for bulk liquids even in horsedrawn days. Early problems with tanks concerned joining the panels or sections securely and making them leakproof. Attaching the tank to the chassis was also a major source of irritation, because of the racking and twisting that takes place on rough roads. The mounting has to be secure, but not too rigid; it has also to attach the whole of the tank which carries the load, not just the part where it meets the chassis.

The materials used in tank construction have changed over the years. Gone are the rivetted and caulked mild steel variety of rectangular section tanks. Also behind us are the copper and the glass-lined types for foodstuffs. Stainless steel and plastics are used today much more widely than even in the 1950s.

The shape of tankers has changed over the years, from the original rectangular and plain cylindrical, to elliptical, double conical, maximum section, D-shaped, tapered, stepped and even back to rectangular, only this time in g.r.p. (glass reinforced plastic).

Tanker shape is dictated by the load to be carried and the method of discharge. What suits an inert powder is no good for beer. Similarly, a cement bulker is unsuitable for fuel.

In the 1950s, most tanker fleets were of plain design so far as shape is concerned. Pressure tanks were cylindrical, fuel tanks either elliptical, D-shape or maximum section. For foodstuffs, glass-lined or stainless steel tanks were usual, with rubber and other special interior coatings for toxic chemicals. Loads which had to be temperature controlled were usually lagged with cork, metal foil or mineral wool, with an outer covering of aluminium for the sake of their appearance.

Bulkers for grain, flour, pellets and powders have undergone extensive development over the past few years. Early types were used for grain and were simple box affairs, loaded through the top and discharged by way of a hole in the floor. Later, with the development of high pressure hydraulic rams, it was possible to arrange tipping discharge. Others have had screw discharge, air blower and combination designs. By the 1950s, cement was being handled both in cylindrical tanks and in rectangular hoppers with tipping, blowing and bottom discharge being tried.

While the maximum capacity tanker is ideal for the delivery of bulk loads of fuel, the handling of lubricating oils is best made by smaller vehicles because of the tiny quantities which, in comparison, are involved. Note that this 1946 Austin tanker of wartime design has no fewer than five compartments, even though the total capacity is no more than 1000 gallons.

From their headquarters in Chippenham, Wiltshire, Bulwark transport operate a large fleet of tankers carrying a wide variety of liquids. This CX 7 Albion rigid eight is a 1949 machine with a tank of about 3000 gallons capacity, operating within the old maximum gross weight of 24 tons. It is pictured passing through Penzance in 1957.

In prewar days, large articulated vehicles were not as common as they are today. Pioneered by Thornycroft in 1898, they were really exploited by Scammell in the 1920s. The 1938 Leyland Beaver articulated tanker shown here was not produced in any quantity, being far more popular as a rigid chassis. This outfit has a rather special shrouded tank for the transport of electrical oils marketed by W. B. Dick, and is carried on BTC 'four-in-line' running gear.

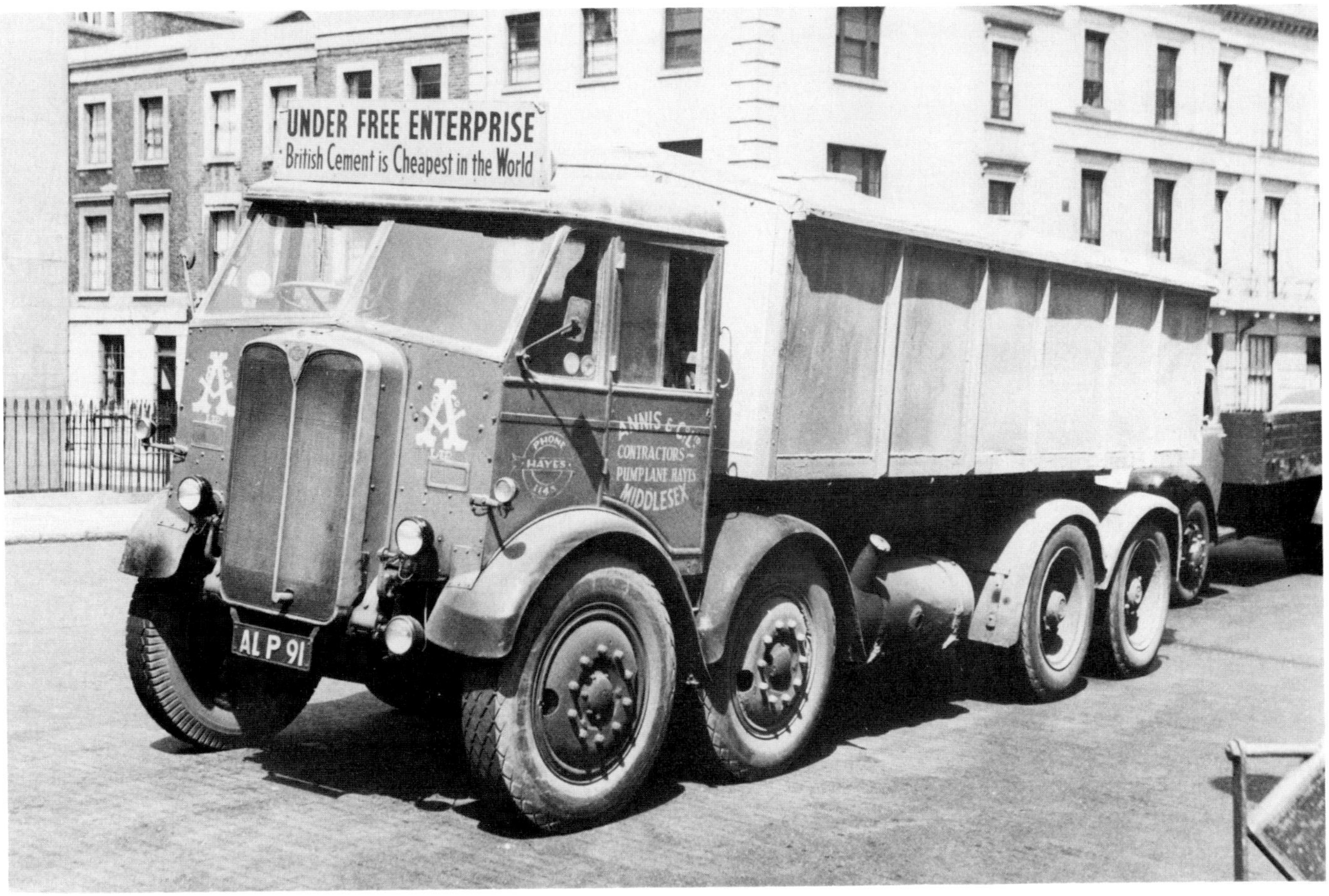

The heavy lorry of the 1930s has that rather period appearance probably because of the high-mounted radiator and the large 40×8 tyre equipment which amply filled the mudwings. This early example of the AEC four-axle model probably started life as a general haulage vehicle, the owners subsequently fitting the bulk body for cement as the demand grew in the postwar building boom.

As a temporary expedient for bulk cement handling, the Cement Marketing Company used some of its Foden tippers with a sheet over the load. This method was acceptable for short runs in fine weather, but was fraught with danger in heavy rain. Totally enclosed rectangular bulkers and, later, pressure tankers were found to be the ideal containers for the cargo, which must be kept perfectly dry.

Davis Brothers (Haulage) Ltd, quickly built up a large undertaking in the late 1950s after requiring ex-BRS units. Traffics included the 'general goods' category, plus quite a large tanker fleet operating both for hire and on contract work. A wide variety of vehicles was included in the fleet, with tankers on AEC, Albion, Leyland and Scammell chassis. The small lettering on the cab side details the locations of the many depots owned.

The petroleum industry was responsible for the growth of many industries which used the valuable commodity as their raw material. Many chemicals, gases and plastics have come on to the market in recent years and many require special handling. The widespread use of LPG has demanded special designs of tankers for its safe transport, because of the high pressures involved. The Albion of Bulwark Transport, pictured on a public weighbridge in Cornwall, was one of the early designs for carrying butane.

CROW CARRYING CO LTD
T.205.A.
SCAMMELL
4095 HK

◄ The Crow Carrying Company is an old established east London haulier which has specialised in tanker operation. It is now part of the Transport Development Group and is located in Silvertown, but was originally based in nearby Barking. In this picture, one of their fleet of Scammells negotiates a roundabout on a hot summer's day in 1959, with the driver enjoying the benefit of the old-style opening windscreen.

Pickfords is probably best known ► for its heavy haulage operations, and for those of its removals department. It also managed to build up a considerable fleet of tankers for the transport of bulk liquids, and this fleet was known as Pickfords Tank Haulage. Quite a number were operated on a regular contract basis and the vehicle illustrated is in the fleet colours of the Fina Petroleum Company. Note the painted number plate, a feature of Pickford's fleet which enabled contract vehicles to be easily identified by sharp-eyed enthusiasts!

With fifteen tons of bulk cement, this HD57 Albion requires bottom gear for the sharp turn and climb from the 'Halt' sign after leaving the cement works at Stone in Kent. The Hall & Co. fleet was usually of good appearance; this eight-wheeler seems to have had a recent mishap to the offside ► corner.

In prewar days, most local authorities burned household refuse as the cheapest way of disposal. The postwar demands for cleaner city air put paid to all that, so producing a demand for the bulk transfer of refuse to distant burial grounds. A. Pannell Ltd of Golders Green had the experience of refuse vehicle contracts behind them, so were well placed to handle this task. Quite a large fleet of AEC Mammoth Major Mk III eight-wheelers with high side bulk bodies were employed in the daily clearance of refuse from central London to pits in Buckinghamshire.

When, in 1954, Guy decided to go 'up market' with a four-axle chassis, they adopted some AEC Mammoth Major components and added the design of cab illustrated. Originally named Goliath, the range was quickly changed to Invincible to avoid confusion with the German manufacturer of the same name.

One of the mainstays of wartime transport was the Bedford in both rigid and tractor forms. This OXC has just been returned to the old style of Shell Mex and BP livery of red, green and black with gold lettering, after wearing the wartime grey of the Pool petrol.

The Foden DG eight-wheel chassis was widely used in long wheelbase form as a trunk haulage vehicle, while the short wheelbase model was equally popular as the basis for tippers. The one pictured has the old style high-sided timber body for the cartage of coke or clinker. Both the style of bodywork and the load were soon to disappear as boilers were converted to oil fuel and timber bodies were replaced by those of metal construction.

CHARRINGTONS
CHARRINGTONS
Mobil
DISTRIBUTORS
1551
1551
VYL 929

Thornycroft eight-wheelers were never so prolific as those from AEC, Foden, ERF, Leyland, Guy and Scammell. While the earlier 1950s models were of usual Thornycroft appearance, some of the later products appeared with a succession of unusual cabs. The cab illustrated is of the type that was current while the Basingstoke factory was in full swing, but those that were cabbed by Boalloy and Alfred Miles were completely at odds with the accepted face of the marque.

Postwar Leyland Beaver and trailer operated by the South Eastern Gas Board for carrying liquid tar from gasworks to tar spraying contractors in London and the south-east. The Metro name on the cab door relates back to pre-nationalisation days when the local gas undertaking was known by that name, for the convenience of its customers.

In the days before pressurised tankers for flour, grain and powders, the logical step after handling in sacks was the gravity discharge bulker. This model 68 ERF of Hills & Partridge of Aylesbury has a bulk body which is loaded through the roof and discharged by tipping. The 18-foot wheelbase chassis is powered by the legendary Gardner 6LW engine.

Wincanton Transport and Engineering had its origins back in the 1920s as a subsidiary of the West Surrey Dairy Co., hauling bulk loads of milk from country collection points to central bottling depots. The rather plain livery was relieved only by the WTE symbol on the cab, and the fleet name on the door. This is *Curlew*, a Mark III AEC Mammoth Major seen at Newport, South Wales in 1958.

Annis & Co. of Pump Lane, Hayes, Middlesex are probably better known for their heavy haulage operations. They did, however, have a reputation for rebuilding and converting vehicles for the specific use, and this eight-wheel cement bulker is one such vehicle, being one of the first bulk cement hoppers on contract for Blue Circle Cement.

Brewers and Millers

Historically successful businesses — beer and bread have long been popular commodities — the brewers and millers have been well able to afford the best equipment. Thus it follows that their vehicles have been of the best order, with the brewers coming out on top with regard to publicising themselves by way of attractive delivery fleets making calls at equally attractive public houses. The two industries also have a connection because of barley being malted and used in the preparation of beer.

Both brewers and millers were, in their early history, local industries. With the course of time, they have become companies, combines and industrial groups. Of course, this has led to a reduction in the number of individual names, with a resulting loss of identity as the groups become larger.

In the early postwar years the ownership position was roughly the same as that of the 1930s, with many hundreds of independent brewers and millers throughout Britain. However, there was a fair amount of inter-trading, particularly with the brewers, added to which certain 'brews' such as Guinness, Bass and Worthington, were bottled by independent bottlers for sale in the houses of various brewers. The millers usually sold flour to bakers anyway, so one did not know whose or what wheat was being used in the loaves.

For all this, the 1950s fleets were varied. Colour schemes, names, brands, lettering and slogans there were in profusion, together with a wide choice of chassis makers and body styles being used. One brewer might prefer to use a flat truck and merely sheet the load, while another might require a roofed vehicle to keep the rain off his bottles.

J. W. Green of Luton were not large brewers in comparison with the big groups of today, but they were progressive none the less. This Commer articulated outfit was one of a fleet for carrying bottled beers from Luton to depots at Stratford, Grantham and Tunbridge Wells. The smooth appearance of the van semi-trailer is matched by the locally-built Commer tractor, and the van roof has a sliding portion for loading from above.

REID'S STOUT
WATNEYS
WATNEYS
A.2
109 כשר
KOSHER BUTCHER   M.SH
CGY 35

◄ As far back as the 1920s, brewers Watney, Combe Reid & Co. included tankers in their fleet with the design of a giant beer barrel which was both functional and eye-catching. The polished wood covering hid the insulated inner truck, and the vehicles were used to cary bulk supplies from brewery to bottling depot. In later years, the use of bulk tanks extended to that of supplying cellar tanks in public houses.

One of the prewar ERF ► eight-wheel vans used by BRS in East Anglia for transport of bagged malt for the London brewers. The body and cab are of light-weight construction by Duramin Engineering, who were one of the leading exponents of all-metal construction based on aluminium alloy sections. Note the unusual three-piece windscreen, often used in cabs by Duramin.

Not much load security is evident with this Thornycroft lorry and trailer loaded with barrels of Guinness. The outfit is part of the Thomas Allen fleet, which had the Guinness contract for the Park Royal brewery for many years, and was photographed outside the old British Mercedes Benz depot in Grosvenor Road, London, where many vehicles parked for the transport cafe opposite. ►

The postwar range of Leyland Beaver, Steer, Hippo and Octopus all shared the style of cab seen on this 1954 Hippo for Watneys. The new, streamlined cab with a mesh grille was a far cry from the prewar style with a prominent exposed cast aluminium radiator, which had been the Leyland image for very many years.

Although this 1953 Leyland Hippo has the original style of radiator and scuttle, the remainder of the cab is of special design, probably by Duramin. It gives the appearance of being an ultra-long wheelbase model, which, when fully laden with bottled beer as on this occasion in June 1951, creaked and groaned as it was reversed over the varying slope of road and adjacent loading bay.

The Hovis fleet was always immaculate in its white and beige livery, and none more so than this fine example of the Foden FG of 1948. Pictured at the Hovis mills in Battersea, this vehicle was of the dual-purpose type for the transport of grain, either bagged or in bulk. It was not the first of this type, however, for Hovis operated several grain bulkers in prewar days, including the impressive Leyland Rhino.

No doubt because of the quality of their products, both Dennis and Thornycroft could number many brewers among their satisfied customers. They offered a wide choice of chassis in the 2-ton to 6-ton load bracket right through to the 1950s, but the market changed somewhat in the next decade and many orders were lost to the products from Longbridge and Dagenham and Luton. The 1936 Thornycroft Dandy pictured here was one in the fleet of Georges Brewery of Bristol.

WHEAT
FOR SNOWDROP FLOUR
A.H. ALLEN & Co LTD CROYDON
A.H. ALLEN & Co LTD
Flour Millers
CROYDON.
SCAMMELL
EVB 53

◄ This Scammell drawbar bulk grain hopper was an unusual vehicle in London. Operated by a Croydon miller, it was used to collect grain in bulk from London docks. The bulker trailer was probably built by Multiwheeler for operation with a Beardmore or Latil tractor prewar, and the Scammell ballast box tractor could be a converted articulated type.

This photograph shows two of the ► small fleet of GV electrics run by Meux & Co., brewers of Nine Elms, just south of the Thames. They were limited to deliveries in the local area. Originally on solid rubber tyres, the electrics were originally in the service of Whitbreads, who changed them to pneumatics and enclosed some of the cabs in the 1930s.

This 1950 model Leyland Steer carries a van body for the transport of bagged malt from maltings to brewers. Rated at 15 tons gross weight, the four-wheel steering type was provided for those operators wanting a load carrier that could carry the maximum payload and yet not have the front axles overloaded should the load not be evenly distributed. There has recently been a resurgence of interest in the design for retail beer delivery. ►

This Scammell rigid eight operated by BRS in the east of England was used to carry malt from the maltings of Norfolk and Suffolk to the London breweries. The large advertisement on the van's sides was about the nearest thing any British vehicle came to the travelling billboards of the United States.

Sporting what must be one of the longest bonnets seen on a British truck, this AEC Majestic and trailer is pictured near one of the regular transport cafes, opposite Battersea Power Station. The vehicle is one of several owned by Joseph Rank, flour millers, who, a little earlier, had also run Foden steamers and Swiss Saurers.

A fully loaded Leyland Comet stands ready at the City Brewery, Exeter. The Comet was an unusual vehicle to find in a retail delivery fleet, even at a brewery. Other types in the Norman and Pring fleet included Austin, Dennis and larger Leylands, including some obtained second-hand from other breweries.

1920s Orwell battery electric truck built by Ransomes, Sims & Jefferies. This heavyweight in the electric vehicle field was well suited to the local delivery of beer in bulk for Watneys, the brewers. They were originally built with open-fronted cabs and solid tyres, but were updated in the 1930s.

Built to the high standards with which this manufacturer was credited, the Dennis Max was a popular machine with both brewers and millers. Three basic models were on offer with the Dennis O·4 engine, plus a further four models with the O·6 engine in the Max 6 range. Later in the 1950s an eight-litre engine was also available.

The rather conservative world of brewers and beer was rather taken aback in the 1950s when the little known brewing company of J. W. Green of Luton acquired the Stratford-on-Avon based Flower and Sons and decided to adopt a new image at the same time. To the surprise of many, the Flowers name was chosen as the trading title of the new venture and a completely new product was launched — the famous Flower's Keg Bitter. Fleet livery was a delicate shade of yellow and included Bedford, Commer, Maudslay, AEC and Thornycroft, plus the distinctive Sentinel six-wheeler shown here.

H. & G. Simonds of Reading was
a medium-sized brewer with
many houses in the surrounding
area. They also supplied beer in
bulk to contract bottlers such as
Robert Porter of Kings Cross,
London, which is where this 1949
ERF model 6·6 is unloading its
60-barrel load. The Simonds fleet
was always well turned out in its
bright red and gold livery.

Guinness of Park Royal Brewery
do not bottle their stout, relying
instead on the bottling facilities of
other brewery companies. This
CX3 Albion was one of the large
fleet of tankers used to move the
stout in bulk to contract bottlers.

The Larger Loads

To some enthusiasts, the most glamorous aspect of road transport is that of the large heavy haulage outfits which grind along on their mammoth tasks with dignity and a leisurely pace. These trucks and their loads attract much publicity because they are usually the heaviest, longest or biggest movers to date. They also embrace some of the largest and most expensive pieces of equipment, all of which is pretty interesting stuff.

The history of the heaviest load movers has gone through the stages of horse, steam, petrol and diesel prime movers, and has often seemed to be rather backward with regard to the trucks used. For instance, they were still using steam when petrol engines were well developed, and hung on to solid-tyred trailers in the face of many years' experience with pneumatics on heavy trucks. But there was sound reasoning behind these seemingly backward viewpoints; the equipment available to the very heaviest end of the market did not attract the development which it deserved. Of course, the pace has quickened since the 1960s, and heavy haulers now have a choice of some very sophisticated equipment, enabling them to handle some very heavy loads indeed.

In the late 1940s and early 1950s, the British market was dominated by such operators as Pickfords Heavy Haulage and Robert Wynn & Sons, with a number of smaller hauliers handling some of the lesser loads. Names which come to mind include: Parks of Portsmouth, Beck & Pollitzer, Cliffords, E. W. Rudd, Thackers & Saltergate, Siddle Cook, Dallas, Hallett Silberman, Fred Edlin, Eastern General, Hauliers Ltd and Edward Box.

For some loads, a heavy duty tractor and a low-loader with a payload of around 25 tons was sufficient. This could handle many of the 'lighter' heavy loads such as a crane base, boiler, bulldozer, transformer or small excavator or parts of ships, and it was usual to have a winch on the trailer, plus a detachable axle, to help with loading. For handling something longer, a ballast box tractor plus a couple of bogies would suffice, but it was when the really heavy and large items were met that specialised tractors and trailers had to be used. Two or more powerful tractors were required for the really heavy lumps, such as steel castings, large transformers, railway locomotives, parts for petrochemical plant, and the like, and the route also might mean additional power requirements. The trailers were also special affairs with facilities for supporting the load from the ends or sides if required, plus partial dismantling to enable loading to take place.

To many truck enthusiasts, the spirit of heavy haulage in the 1950s was effectively captured by the fleet of US Army Pacific tank transporter tractors used by Wynns of Newport in South Wales. Skillfully rebuilt in the company's workshops, the Pacifics usually operating in pairs, could be seen on most of the major heavy moves of the period. The Crane trailer is also typical of the equipment in use at that time.

The Scammell has been in the forefront of heavy haulage operation in Britain for very many years. Here we see a pair of 'Pioneers' in the Pickfords fleet, tackling a long hill on the North Circular Road at Finchley, north London, with a fractionating column bound for Coryton Refinery. Note that the bogies are the old solid-tyre variety.

Mobilgas
PICKFORDS
MLF 22
CORYTON REFINERY

The term heavy haulage can embrace rather diverse loads, for the operation does not always revolve around boilers and transformers, although they often qualify as the heaviest or the largest; nor does the equipment have to be of the exotic and expensive type, as demonstrated by this Annis ERF eight-wheeler with swivelling bolster on the body to take the front end of this load. A simple 'dolly' consisting of a pair of oscillating axles is used to support the rear end of the pre-stressed concrete beams.

Sunters of Consett were well placed to handle some of the loads which were produced by the steel works of the County Durham area. Employing plain equipment, the company handled all types of heavy and outsize traffic using Foden, Scammell and Leyland tractors with a variety of flat, low-loader and well trailers together with bogies and bolsters as required.

Pickfords had many ballast box
Scammells in their fleet which
could adequately handle jobs
such as this boiler in their stride.
The Crane trailer has a detachable
rear axle and a winch to facilitate
loading, and a variety of loose
tools and equipment would be
carried to carry out the necessary
jacking, packing and winching
required in loading or positioning
the load at its destination.

The Caterpillar scraper just about
fits on this articulated low loader
in the Sunter fleet, and, except for
its width, hardly qualifies as
anything special in road haulage.
It was photographed on the layby
at South Mimms, whose parking
facilities and nearby cafe made it
a regular staging post for heavies
on the A1 road north of London.

◄ Pictured just after acquisition by BRS — note the stencilled fleet number — this Vulcan artic, with low loader trailer is not quite typical of heavy haulage operations of the period. The small bucket excavator is almost a period piece in itself, although it is diesel powered and not steam, as one might think.

In some respects the heavy haulage specialists were slow to make changes in their method of operation and the equipment they used. The heavy lump of machinery, being moved by this 1943 ex-E. W. Rudd Scammell in May 1955, is on a very old solid-tyred trailer, a far cry from the sophisticated power steered, air suspended, radial-tyred units of today.

Pictured in Nine Elms Lane is this ERF 5·4 model tractor of Otway and Golder, a firm specialising in the transport of plant and heavy equipment to the construction industry. The Hands low-loader with 'knock-out' axle is loaded with an old Ransomes & Rapier mobile crane, a type that was very popular in docks and warehouses for handling moderate loads in the days before the widespread ◄ adoption of fork trucks.

PICKFORDS
PICKFORDS
AJD 682
G.F.DREW
yland

Local Delivery

Most local delivery trucks are taken for granted, both by the enthusiasts and the public at large. In the eyes of the truck buff, they are rather mundane affairs, usually in the light to medium class, and normally consist of just a plain box body on a mass produced chassis.

Yet, if one looks closer, the picture is not quite so bland, for this sector of the transport industry is the largest and most important in terms of design and cost – representing a huge chunk of the total distribution cost and, therefore, the final price of the commodity to 'Joe Public'.

Admittedly, there is not much on the surface to warrant the need to single out this section for particular emphasis, but the trucks used continue to receive attention by chassis and body designers all the time. It is merely the lack of glamour and publicity which fails to get them noticed. Yet, they are of the utmost importance for the daily delivery tasks of all our everyday needs to the countless thousands of retail shops and markets.

The local delivery truck of the 1950s was basically smaller than those in use today. The loads carried were in the main all stacked by hand, for these were early days in mechanical handling and the most widespread form of mechanisation was the ubiquitous sack truck. It should be mentioned though that these were the days of comparatively cheap labour, and some delivery vehicles worked with a driver's mate or van boy to help with the 'humping'. In most cases the load had to go into and out of the body over the tailboard, for there were few bodies with side doors. There were a few trades which went to the expense of special features on their trucks to help with load stacking, such as racking to store trays of cakes or heavily insulated bodies for the transport of ice cream and roof rails for hanging garments, but in the main everything was stacked on the floor.

There was little in the way of specialised equipment, for fork trucks and palletisation was in its infancy, hydraulic tail-lifts were yet to come, the shrink-wrapping of loads was unknown and the curtain-sided van was in the development stage.

Experiments were taking place to discover the ideal local delivery truck, which to many of us means a box van, but while that design may suffice for many applications, it is not the complete answer. So detail changes were being made.

A bonnetted layout produced a rather long vehicle for a given load space, so forward control was a logical progression. Access to a box van means heavy and expensive doors or rolling shutters, so curtain sides were tried. The protrusion of the engine into the forward control cab made cross cab movement difficult, so below floor engines were tried. A standard cab means no access to the body direct from the cab, so integral cab/body designs were produced. Continual dismounting through wide hinged cab doors is tiresome and often difficult, so why not try sliding doors? The driver complains of having to reach up high to get at the load, so in order to lower the body height, it was necessary to use smaller diameter wheels. Another idea was to use an articulated, low-platform trailer, but this increased the overall length, although it gave a certain degree of flexibility.

Bodywork of the period included metal panelling on a framework of either wood or metal sections. Metal-faced plywood, which gave a better interior finish, was also used. The roof panels were usually metal panels, or even timber boards or plywood panels with a fabric covering. Some smaller vans merely had a fabric roof stretched over strips of timber. Roof lights were small.

The frozen foods and vegetables revolution was just beginning in the 1950s and most vans relied upon thick insulating panels and dry ice (solid carbon dioxide) for keeping the products cold. Refrigeration plants were large and expensive.

◀ It seems ironical that British Railways, which was so opposed to road transport, should possess one of the largest road vehicle fleets in the country, albeit engaged on local collection and delivery services. The Dennis Pax illustrated was operated by the Western Region and was finished in the Mars livery, for BR distributed their products from the Slough factory.

Not really typical of the contract fleet operated by BRS from their Searles Road, south London depot is this prewar Bedford WT furniture van. Note that the cryptic note on the windscreen says '6am Mon', obviously put there by the driver who does not want to be hemmed in among the large number of newspaper vans which used to be garaged at the depot just visible in the background. ▶

BATCHELARS
BATCHELARS of CROYDON
FURNISHERS of DISTINCTION. EST. 1834.
REMOVALS & WAREHOUSING.
DIAL CROYDON 6171
IG 7396

Widely used by the railways for their local services, the Scammell Mechanical Horse was adopted by many other users where the high degree of manoeuvrability and the speedy change of trailers made them ideal. J. Ward & Sons used this example for retail deliveries of meat. It was handy in the confined spaces of Smithfield Meat Market and an ideal size for hauling the standard insulated lift van containers.

The introduction of the Bedford S-type 7-tonner provided very many operators with the opportunity to obtain a vehicle in the payload class that up to then had been the province of Dennis, Dodge and Seddon. The Bedford illustrated was one of the first to go into service with BRS at Blackwall Tunnel depot, and it would be followed by many more in both rigid and articulated form.

The very large transport fleet of caterers J. Lyons & Co., included a wide variety of both chassis manufacturers and body types. In the 1950s, one could see AEC, Albion, Bedford, Commer, Ford, Leyland, Morris, Thornycroft, Karrier and Guy. The Guy Wolf illustrated was based at Cadby Hall, Kensington and used for the delivery of cakes and swiss rolls to the very many shops and restaurants owned by Lyons at that time.

Pictured against the blitzed buildings in the City of London is one of the small fleet of Latil four-wheel steering tractors operated by British Railways for certain special applications. This example was operated by the Southern Region for handling the special heavy containers on the type of low-loading trailer shown. Other BR Regions used the Latils with bolster trailers for long loads or for towing the unusual road/rail tankers for beer transport.

The old AEC drawbar tractor illustrated probably started life as a much larger trunk vehicle in the fleet of Bouts Tillotson of Waterden Road, Stratford. Now owned by BRS, it was used to shunt trailers in the yard as well as taking them to delivery points where it would be difficult for the trunk vehicle to gain access, or because the trailer load was for a different destination.

Unusual in the field of delivery vehicles was this little Albion of the Star Laundry of east London. Even though it is of forward control design with just a half-height cab door, it does appear over engineered for its capacity of about 2 tons.

Bedford middle-weights with drawbar trailers have never been a common sight, but this outfit is on rather short distance work, moving boxed tomatoes from growers to dockside in Guernsey. Note the unusual cab which was built by Neville as a forward control conversion for bonnetted trucks, such as the Bedford.

Vehicle designers are constantly looking at ways of improving delivery vehicles in order to make them more efficient. Easy-access cabs, low load stacking, better access to the load, load security and mechanical handling are all areas of design requiring attention. In the 1950s, both Albion and Dennis looked at the problems. Dennis produced the Stork, while Albion introduced their Claymore, of which an example is shown. Note that the load is palletised and an early design of curtain side is provided, while the engine is beneath the floor.

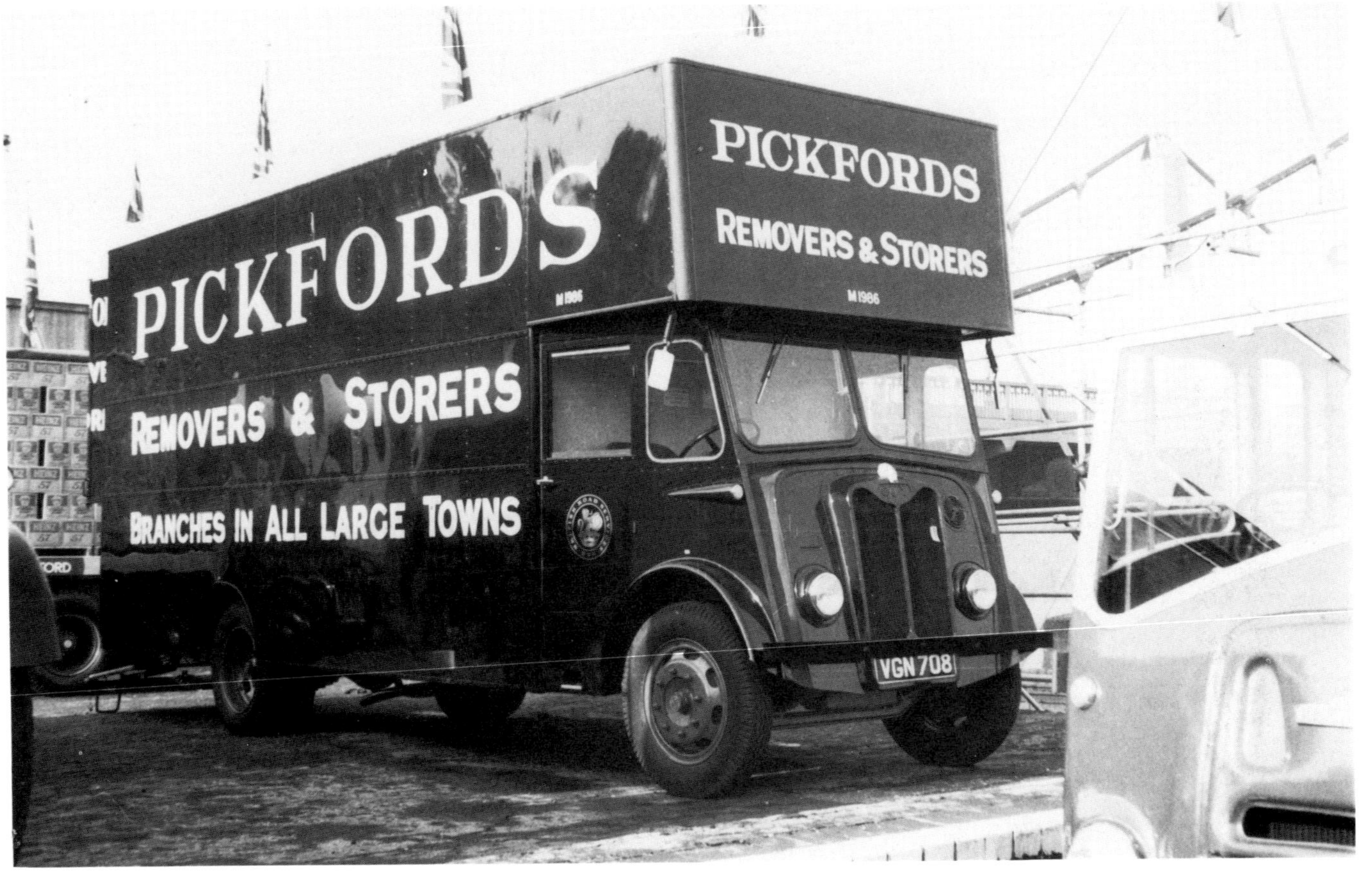

For very many years the Pickfords Removals fleet contained many Bedfords, but, after its absorption into the Special Traffics Division of the Road Haulage Executive, there was a change of policy. The Guy Vixen chassis was chosen as the basis of the replacement fleet and the scuttle fabricated from g.r.p. panels. Bodywork was kept within the Executive, being produced by the bodybuilding division.

The Pax was the most successful model for Dennis Brothers in the postwar years, selling in large numbers to the municipal market as a medium truck as well as forming the basis for special refuse types. It was also very popular for local delivery with co-operative societies and many brewers. The six-wheel model pictured here is very much a special type with 15-inch wheels to obtain a low loading height.

Ever since Henry Ford had striven to launch his £100 car and bring motoring to the millions, the Ford name has tended to reflect the cheaper end of the market. This point of view extended to trucks as well as cars, and Ford doggedly strove to shrug off this image by gradually extending their range upwards. The Thames Trader pictured illustrates the tasks that they could handle, the bucket excavator making quite an impressive load.

One of the success stories in the truck world is undoubtedly that of the Scammell Mechanical Horse and later Scarab series of medium-weight articulated outfits. With the Scammell design of instantaneous coupling, the little three-wheeler won sales in the municipal fleets and with the railways. A 1952 Scarab operating out of Kings Cross depot of Eastern Region is illustrated.

James and Son of south London is an old established company which specialises in the clearance of spent grains from breweries for conversion into cattle feed. In the early postwar years, they added this Ford 7V to their fleet for operation with an older trailer, a very unusual combination for this type of truck. Earlier vehicles in the James fleet had included a fine choice of Foden steam wagons and later Reo Speed Wagons, all operating with drawbar trailers.

Dodge had enjoyed reasonable sales for their trucks in Britain for many years. Originally directly imported, they were subsequently assembled at Kew and then ultimately built in Britain completely. The forward-control model pictured here was a demonstrator for this new model introduced in 1957.

This style of forward-control Morris Commercial was introduced in 1949 and was originally fitted with the Swiss Saurer diesel engine. It was subsequently engined by a Nuffield diesel. The one pictured was in the service of the BBC, and is seen loading scenery at the old Alexandra Palace Studios. Note the dangerous front-opening cab doors.

The high cubic capacity required for furniture removal vans usually entailed using the longest wheelbase chassis available, and, yet, the normal control layout was liked because of the cab space required for both driver and porters, but, as shown by this picture of a Ford 7V for Freeborns of north London, it did not always follow. This vehicle must have been rather warm in the summer with the V-8 petrol engine protruding into the cab space, making it rather cramped for any more than two crew.

TATE & LYLE
Sugar Refiners
LONDON
145
144

There was an acute shortage of all vehicles during World War Two with the majority of truck production going to the military. A few essential industries were helped with new vehicles, including some supplied from the United States under the Lease-Lend scheme. The International Harvester KB series was allocated for such diverse operations as fire fighting, bomb damage clearance and, as those illustrated for Tate & Lyle, food supplies.

The Loadstar was the redesigned progression of the Austin K range of bonnetted middle-weight trucks in the 1950s. It was a popular machine and sold well against the Bedford, Commer and Ford competition. This particular example carries a Luton van body which appears as high as it is long!

The old railway companies were continually trying to improve their rolling stock fleets, both on the rails and on the road. This policy continued with British Railways who took an exhibition of both types of rolling stock round the country during a 1958 publicity campaign. This Austin delivery truck with BMC diesel engine and unusual plastics cab was among a display of trailers, bulkers, demountables and the latest in palletisation techniques.

◄Much publicity was given to the new 'Big Bedford' when it was introduced in 1950, for it was the first Bedford truck with forward control and marked a further step up the payload ladder with its 7-ton capacity. It was to prove a popular machine, and diesel engine versions followed, first with proprietary engines and later with Bedford's own. The photograph shows quite a rare drawbar combination, which allowed more bulky boilers to be handled per journey.

When British Road Services ordered a fleet of standard vans for parcels work, they asked the staff for suggestions at the design stage. The result was the Austin 5-ton parcel van illustrated, which used the standard normal control chassis but with a suitably modified front end to enable the maintenance staff better access to the engine. Sliding doors were fitted to the cab, and a half width bulkhead was installed for front ▼access to the load.

The old Lyons vans were painted in an attractive dark blue, white and gold livery, which made them stand out in the traffic of the day. Bodywork of J. Lyons vehicles was carried out by Normand Ltd, of Park Royal, a Lyons subsidiary. Notice that this Guy Wolf has a heavily insulated body with separate doors for each compartment containing various items from the range of Lyons' Ice Cream.   ►

LYONS ICE CREAM
LYONS
ICE CREAM
J. LYONS & C..
CADBY HALL
LONDON, W.14
5095
EXK 615

TATE & LYLE
Sugar Refiners
TATE & LYLE
Sugar Refiners
LONDON   LIVERPOOL
EJJ 821
& LYLE
r Refiners

The twin-steer design of six-wheeler was pioneered by ERF, but was rapidly copied by Leyland with their twin-steer Beaver, AEC with their Mustang and Foden with the DG. Tate & Lyle used to operate quite a number of Fodens, including eight-wheelers on shop deliveries!

One of the criticisms levelled against the three-wheel Mechanical Horse design was its instability in certain circumstances. This led certain users to opt for a four-wheel design of light articulated vehicle, which could still couple to the trailers made so popular by the instantaneous couplings designed in the 1930s. The Eastern Region of British Railways was the operator of the Jen-Tug illustrated, which was built by Jensen Motors using an Austin A40 engine. A battery electric version was also on offer, with electrical equipment by Hindle, Smart & Co. — the Jen-Helecs.

The Leyland Comet was the medium-weight contender from this particular manufacturer, and the first model to receive such dramatic treatment of front end styling at that time. Barretts Sweets of Wood Green were the operators of this one, pictured beneath the now demolished railway bridge at Noel Park Station, north London.

A rather unusual van for delivering new furniture, a DG Foden, probably operated by a haulage contractor in the name of the furniture manufacturer. As furniture is comparatively bulky for its weight, furniture vans tend to be mounted on the less expensive mass produced chassis like Bedford, Commer, Ford and Dodge. The vehicle following closely, one of the large milk tankers fleet operated by Wincanton Transport and Engineering for the dairy industry, transporting in bulk from country creameries to town bottling depots, is one of several Albion Caledonian eight-wheelers then current.

This Morris Series III appears to be a Rowntree delivery van, but close inspection reveals that it is owned and operated by British Railways, Western Region. Until 1948, distribution of Rowntree products was made by N.M.U. Ltd, who were absorbed into the British Road Services operations. Subsequently, along with many products distributed on a nation-wide basis, the operation was handled by British Railways, and some vehicles had the chocolate and gold livery.

This Thames ET6 van was used for the retail delivery of evaporated milk. It is painted in the red and white livery adopted by Carnation, but it was owned and operated on their behalf by Caledonian Road Services.

A typical removal van of the period is this 3-ton Bedford WT model, which was of ample capacity for the contents of many small flats and terraced houses. The normal control layout gave a reasonable three-man cab, and the tailboard/hinged flap arrangement at the rear could cope with those little extras like bikes, sacks of coal or the occasional wardrobe. Note the bold lettering on the van which was rather less than could be seen on some vans, often with the addition of slogans or even full colour paintings.

Lightweights

Right at the bottom of the market for trucks come the very lightest of the load carriers. This is the realm of the small delivery van and the pick-up, the world of the High Street and the service industries.

In the postwar days, there was a considerable variety of light trucks available, much the same as today, the main difference being that they were mostly British.

Many of the British volume car producers had added a light van or truck to their range, using the running gear and front end of the current passenger carrier. Some also used a suitable engine for both a production car and a light truck in their commercial range. In most instances, the car and its van counterpart went under different names.

Austin had their car-derived GV range of 10-cwt payload models, plus the K8 3-way van, which was for 25-cwt loads. Morris was always in the same arena, having car-based Z and Y vans, while Morris Commercial marketed their forward control J type 10-cwt and the larger 15-cwt PV, which was later replaced by the LD.

Ford was a front runner with its E04C 5-cwt and the 10-cwt E83W, both car derived, and later the 400E forward control with Cortina engine. From Luton in Bedfordshire came the Commers with the rather smart Express 8-cwt (Minx-based) and the larger 15-cwt forward control 1500 van, plus the Bedford JC (later PC) as a 10-cwt car type. Then came the smaller producers such as the 2-cylinder Bradford by Jowett and the 2-stroke Trojan for 15-cwt loads.

Battery electric vans and trucks were plentiful in the choice of producers, but with little variation in capacity. They had very little appeal to the bulk of light van users because of their inherently limited speed and distance performance. They did find buyers in the bakeries, dairies, hospitals, councils and other public undertakings, and the choice of builder included Brush, NCB, Wilson, Helecs, Victor, Electruk, Morrison Electric, Cleco, Douglas, Graiseley and the Q.

◄This Bedford CA truck with outsize beer crate was how one brewery company decided it could attract attention while touring its public houses. A small load space has been created in the middle of the 'crate', and this was used for publicity material. The vehicle often attended carnivals and other public attractions in order to promote a greater awareness for the product.

This prewar Dodge 15-cwt van ► was one of a large fleet of Dodge and Humber vans used by the London *Evening Standard* newspaper for the speedy delivery of papers to the street corner newsvendors. This particular example has been well used, and the original fancy radiator grille has been replaced with something rather more practical for the busy world of newspaper delivery.

DXA 755
EVENING STANDARD
807

The small local delivery van was a natural progression from the boy on his carrier bicycle or three-wheel box trike of earlier days. Austin, Bedford, Ford, Jowett, Commer and Morris held the major share of the market, but there were plenty of other types, including converted cars in use. The 5-cwt capacity Morris shown here on tradeplates has just been sold out of service from London Transport.

As one would expect, some of the electricity supply companies used battery electric vans for their delivery and service fleets. Most were in the 10-cwt to 1-ton payload size, and were made by such firms as NCB, Wilson, Q, Hindle Smart, Victor, Brush and Morrison Electricar. The Q van pictured here was used by the London Electricity Board, but when due for renewal, it was replaced by a petrol engined van!

The trend toward electric trucks for house-to-house milk deliveries had begun in the 1930s, but it was not until the 1950s that the switch had achieved anything like completion. Some were of the pedestrian variety, but a rider type had to be used for larger loads. Driver protection and load security are definitely 1950s style on this little Brush 'Pony' for 10-cwt loads, larger capacities being met by four-wheel trucks by a variety of makers including NCB, Wilson, W & E, Ross, Hindle Smart, Brush, Electruk and Morrison Electricar.

HEDDON COURT PARADE
COCKFOSTERS
KLC 889
EXPRESS
DAIRY

The sort of morning we all fear — icy cold, a two-cylinder Jowett Bradford and a struggling battery! With their two-cylinder horizontally-opposed engine and reversed-layout gear change, these little 5-cwt vans could be quite daunting to anyone reared on bigger four-cylinder engines, but they performed well in sympathetic hands.

Photographed outside Whitechapel Underground Station while attending a breakdown is this example of the E83W Ford 10-cwt van, which was a very popular model in the postwar period. Contemporaries were the Morris Y-type, Austin GV, Bedford JCV and the smaller capacity Commer Supervan.

Something Different

'Something different' can have many meanings to a truck enthusiast. Trucks can be purposely different, such as those produced specifically for advertising or publicity, or they can be different because they are outside the normal production models on offer from the truck builders.

The old motorised beer bottles and toothpaste tubes come into the first category, while the second embraces the minor variations such as additional axles, or the less frequently seen trucks by minor builders such as TVW, Rutland or Union, or those 'one-off' produced for a particular job.

Both aspects seem to become rarer as time goes by. It is more expensive and more difficult to put an advertising vehicle on the road than it used to be, while the very facts that more stringent regulations govern the construction of trucks and that they need to be 'type approved' has removed the little variations to standard productions that could otherwise provide some interesting types.

Not so many years ago there were numerous advertising and publicity trucks about, which helped relieve the drab procession of everyday transport. Some of these were extremely well designed and executed, and luckily the Bass Worthington Daimler Bottle survives, but others have disappeared. Their place today is taken by the numerous replica vintage vans which throng British high streets.

The other view of 'different' is less easily defined, and it varies according to taste. Anything pre-1960 and still working could possibly qualify, together with survivors of defunct makes. Unusual bodywork often gets a second glance, as does an articulated version of a truck that is usually seen only in its rigid form. Other variations include non-standard cabs or unusual axle configurations, such as twin-steering axles.

A few years ago, many trucks sported special cabs, particularly the integral van designs. It was also easy for enterprising operators to rebuild a whole number of trucks to their own liking using proprietary parts; the Union Gold Storage tractors are good examples. Other small truck builders, such as Rowe, Manton, TVW and Argyle all added a welcome variety to the large volume producers. The rebuilding of the Wynn's Pacifics is another instance of a welcome difference, although the appearance of the Heanor Haulage HHTs in recent years does give a glimmer of hope that the next generation will find a few 'just different'.

As mentioned elsewhere in this volume, Watneys the brewers had many barrel-shaped vehicles in their fleet. This one was just a little different for it carried no beer, just publicity material for display in the company public houses. The Commer Raider was finished in a livery of red barrel and black bonnet and wings.

?
JNC 829

Pictured on display after it had been on the Thompson Brothers stand at the 1958 Commercial Motor Show at Earls Court is the experimental Leyland Dromedary integral tanker for BP. Looking extremely futuristic for the period, the design featured a rear-engine position as adopted for the Atlantean bus chassis, Leyland axles suspended from the Thompson tank and a tricky little front door to the cab.

Another brewery idea for an advertising vehicle, this time in the shape of a miniature medieval tower for Red Tower Lager, produced by the Royal Brewery at Manchester. Fabricating bodies of this sort was a long and difficult job, usually requiring a frame and an aluminium covering. The later introduction of plastics and glass fibre helped make such displays a much simpler task.

In an effort to add a touch of individuality to their fleet and gain attention while on deliveries, the South London Brewery used several of these Maudslay Mogul vehicles. Finished in an attractive livery of red with gold lettering, they were certainly distinctive among the more mundane trucks of the period.

During the 1930s, the City of Westminster council took delivery of a fleet of rather unusual articulated battery electric vehicles based on the Scammell design, with Electricar electrical equipment. The reason for buying the electrics was because of the need to collect refuse from the busy West End area during the night when traffic is at a minimum and many residents are sleeping.

Along with scrapyards, the winter premises of showmen and fairground sites during the season are prime locations for keen truck enthusiasts. When vehicles are sold out of service, they often see a second, and often longer, span of activity with one of the travelling showmen. This 1937 Leyland Hippo passed out of meat haulage into the hands of Len Bibby's Amusements transporting his Waltzer on tour.

Quite rare on London's streets was this Unipower four-wheel drive tractor, which was probably acquired for work in the congested dock areas. The drawbar trailer has a low loading height, achieved by the use of large section tyres on small diameter rims, and it embodies the 'four-in-line' design of axles where each pair of wheels is suspended on a short oscillating axle.

Our Business is Your Pleasure.
HERE COMES
LOADS
OF
EVER POPULAR
~WALTZER~
ON TOUR.
LEN BIBBY'S
AMUSEMENTS
ON
Tour.
Nº 2
LEYLAND
EGJ 902

H.V. SMITH & Co LTD
TRINIDAD ASPHALT MACADAM
WORKS·TOTTENHAM & DAGENHAM DOCK
CML 734
CAUTION
TARSPRAYING
DYE 610

The Daimler bottles of Bass Worthington were unmistakable, and rank as the best advertising vehicles of their time. The sleeve-valve engines were very quiet in operation, even if the exhaust was somewhat smoky after a while.

Childhood summers were always enlivened by the arrival of the tar sprayer. In this photograph, a Sentinel DG4 of H. V. Smith & Co. pauses while a fresh supply of tar is pumped from the tanker.

One of the earliest designs of bulk carriers was this type of grain hopper trailer in use with a Shropshire flour mill. It is seen leaving the Mersey Tunnel in 1958. Loading was by way of a hatch in the roof and discharge through the floor. The tractor unit is a 1933 Multiwheeler.

◄ Using parts from Old Fodens, the Union Cartage Co. of Bromley by Bow constructed a number of these drawbar tractors for hauling meat containers from London docks to Smithfields Meat Market. The particular tractor has the radiator from an old Fowler vehicle.

This Manton six-wheeler was one ► of a pair which Finney, Barlow & Co. of Gravesend, Kent, operated in the 1950s. It started life as a petrol-engined Albion, and was extensively rebuilt by Manton Motors, and had a Perkins diesel engine installed.

Sutton and Son (St Helens) Ltd acquired a number of these TVW tractor units from Transport Vehicles (Warrington) after Rolls-Royce sold off the vehicle building interests of Sentinel. A rigid six-wheeler (HDJ 126) was ▼ also in the fleet.

Madeira Drive, Brighton at the end of the 1954 Veteran Car Run, with a 1942 Thornycroft Trusty, which has come to collect one of the entrants. This was before the old vehicle rallies, which form part of the modern enthusiasts' calendar, became so popular. Soon, Brighton's seafront witnessed the long parade of old commercials after the HCVC had inaugurated its own Brighton Run.

Better known for their heavy haulage operations, throughout a long history going back to 1863, Wynns of South Wales had engaged in general haulage, bulk liquids, heavy haulage and timber transport, using in turn horses, steam tractors, petrol lorries and diesel trucks. Photographed in Brecon in July 1958 is one of their ex-American military FWD tractors, fitted with a winch for timber extraction, and towing a pole trailer.

Trucks for Construction

Before construction work can begin, the site has to be prepared and this often involves demolition of old buildings and the levelling of the site. This is the first stage at which trucks make an appearance, for they are involved in getting the brick rubble, broken concrete and scrap ironwork away from the site.

In the clearance of bombed buildings during and after World War Two, fleets of tippers were engaged on the work, and this was repeated in the vast postwar slum clearance and rebuilding schemes in Britain's major cities. For many years, these city areas echoed to the incessant noise of pneumatic drills, bucket loaders and heavy tippers used in the wholesale demolition programme as it ground on. A short pause followed while the planners and surveyors viewed the sites, made their drawings and did their calculations. This was short-lived: there was soon a return to the din of pile drivers, concrete mixers and the seemingly incessant passing of numerous tippers, cement bulkers, steel carriers, aggregate tippers and all manner of truck orientated equipment.

Some of the contracts lasted for months; others ran into years. In these early days of postwar rebuilding, sites had little mechanisation. Tower cranes were in their infancy and cement pumpers unknown. Rough terrain fork trucks did not exist, and the humble wheelbarrow was still in regular use. Little site dumpers scurried around if the surface permitted, and some sites used miniature railway lines to cross the area. Crane carriers were really no more than a road-going chassis with a crane superstructure mounted over the rear bogie. The air compressors were very noisy and the pneumatic drills unshrouded. Site vehicles were invariably late in their life and often never left the site again. The use of ex-military equipment was widespread, not only because it was inexpensive, but because it was often better suited than the civilian types available, where all-wheel-drive was not often found.

Redpath, Brown & Co. of Greenwich were the operators of this classic example of the 1930s Leyland Beaver. Used for carrying steel girders and structural steel sections to building sites, the plain style of body is well braced for heavy work. Note the steel bolster which took the weight of the long steel beams, which often exceeded the length of the lorry.

Foden DG eight-wheel chassis with Smith, Rodley lattice boom crane employed in the fleet of John Mowlem and seen on a piling job at Silvertown, east London, in 1958. This outfit is typical of the period and shows the design of crane carriers of that time, when an adapted road-going chassis was fitted with the superstructure of a convenient boom crane.

Willments of Waterloo were heavily involved in the demolition and reconstruction work in London after the war, when huge areas of the blitzed city were being cleared and new builders erected. They were also involved in work for the 1951 Festival of Britain on the South Bank, and the old Leyland tipper illustrated was one of the many kept busy on the Battersea Park Funfair site.

The Hollman compressor carried by this little Dennis is probably just about enough for this 45-cwt vehicle. Dennis Brothers were not very strong in the construction industry nor in general haulage. They were, in fact, finding good customers in the municipal and brewery fleets of the period.

Dorman, Long & Co. were both manufacturers and suppliers of steel beams and structural steelwork, and as such were very busy in the postwar building schemes for the blitzed areas of Britain's cities. The London-based fleet included both rigid and articulated Thornycrofts for handling the long and heavy loads in the days before reinforced concrete beams become so widely used.

The old established firm of Foden has long been renowned for quality, and its range of trucks has been much admired by enthusiasts. There were mixed feelings when Fodens had to look round for a buyer in the early 1980s and was subsequently taken over by Paccar of the United States. It is difficult to pinpoint the zenith of the Foden truck, but many believe it to be in the 1950s, when the FG six-wheeler shown above was produced.

The Bedford O type gained a reputation for hard work and reliability. This pair, operated by Capon & Sons on the gruelling task of brick carrying to building sites, are pictured ready to leave the London Brick Stewartby works.

Twin-steer Dennis vehicles have been built only in small numbers. The first design was produced just prior to World War Two and the postwar version was titled Max 6, presumably because it had six wheels. But it might have meant six cylinders, for Max 6 was also allocated to the four-wheel model with the larger engine. A few years later, a special twin-steer version of the Centaur was built for Shell Mex & BP, and the Pax V for bulk loads.

◀ Operated by the Eastern Region of British Railways, this ex-military Crossley drawbar tractor was used with a bolster trailer for the carriage of steel girders, large timbers and long reinforcing rods.

▼ George Wimpey & Sons, the civil engineering contractors, were the owners of this 1952 Scammell Pioneer heavy haulage tractor, seen here with a Crane trailer loaded with the base section of a bucket excavator in mid-Wales in 1958. The Pioneer was popular as a heavy tractor in the days before the introduction of the Constructor.

Highlighted by the early morning sun, a DG Foden of the Cement Marketing Company tips a load of raw materials adjacent to the busy steam grab, which feeds it to a long conveyor. The scene is at an old section of the works at Grays, Essex, an area which was always busy with truck traffic. ▶

CEMENT MARKETING COMPANY
PORTLAND CEMENT
MLC 780

In Case of Mishap

The art of vehicle recovery has reached new levels of expertise in recent years, partly because of the need to clear traffic arteries quickly, and partly because the expensive trucks now employed require expert handling in order to minimise further damage.

In the immediate postwar years, vehicles were not so complicated as they are today. Automatic transmission on trucks was unheard of, and most suspensions were of the old steel leaf-spring type. The process of recovery was therefore much simpler, and was often achieved by a straight pull out by another truck, or by running a cable round the overturned vehicle and just winching it out — and without much regard to the bodywork or to possible chassis twisting! Nor were there the number of heavy recovery specialists that exist today. It was often a case of the police calling on the local bus company to come along and tow away the offending truck; they, in turn, would arrive with their old converted bus.

The number of heavy duty ex-military machines which came onto the market (and still do), made a great difference to the vehicle recovery business. For here was a purpose-built, heavy duty unit that had been designed to recover heavy pieces of equipment, which were often in appalling conditions. Even if the purpose-built machine could not be obtained, at least an all-wheel-drive truck could be bought and the specialist equipment added to suit. British AEC Matador and Scammell types, together with American Ward La France and Diamond T recovery trucks can still be found performing good work in dozens of locations.

Not everyone wanted a recovery truck at the heavy end of the market. Thus, all manner of ex-regular service trucks were given a further lease of life by the addition of a hand operated crane and a winch and such items as a rigid towbar, heavy duty jacks, packing blocks and perhaps oxyacetylene cutting equipment.

Some excitement for the local population of North Finchley as they stand to watch the antics of the BRS recovery crew, who have brought along their ageing AEC Majestic to assist the unfortunate Seddon artic driver. A case of too high a speed round a bend was probably the cause of the loaded trailer suddenly breaking away from the tractor and wrenching off the fifth wheel coupling, which is of the old Carrimore pattern. The first task was to release the ropes securing the load and let it fall into the sheet, after which the trailer was righted and towed away by the recovery vehicle and another vehicle and crew sent to pick up the load from the road.

CAPSTAN
BRIXTON
MECHANICAL
148 GF
GGC 756

◄ Most of the American trucks in regular use at the outbreak of war were quickly impressed for emergency war work, so, except for ex-military equipment, American trucks were rather rare in Britain. This Diamond T recovery vehicle working for the old London County Council was one of the few civilian types to be seen around in the 1950s.

The United Service Transport Company used this ex-military Dodge recovery truck for breakdown service for the very large fleet of vans supplied on contract to traders in the London area. The north London depot was located close to Euston Station and serviced the many newspaper vans which ferried newspapers between Fleet Street and the London rail termini. ►

Many of the little Bedford MW 15-cwt trucks found their way into civilian fleets after 1945, and some companies took the trouble to convert them to forward control. This example was equipped with a hand-operated recovery crane for the rescue of London Co-op electric milk and bread vans which had broken down. ▼

overleaf
Many large transport fleets retain a recovery vehicle for their own use, and often this consists of an obsolete fleet vehicle with a crane and other equipment added, frequently by the operator's own workshop staff. This Leyland Beaver of Crosse and Blackwell is one such machine, having served many years of distribution life before being rejuvenated as the company recovery outfit. It often made an appearance at early HCVC rallies in the late 1950s.

LEYLAND
CROSSE & BLACKWELL
BREAKDOWN SERVICE
205 GC
CROSSE &
BLACKWELL

Scrapyards

There is something slightly mystical about scrapyards, almost bordering on the atmosphere of a graveyard, for that is where most vehicles meet their end. To most truck enthusiasts who have a regard for the historical side of the hobby, scrapyards are important places, whether the search is for a complete old vehicle or just some parts for one. Some followers of old trucks thoroughly enjoy a day spent touring round certain locations where interesting yards are known to exist.

Like most other things in life, scrapyards come in a variety of types — large or small, organised or haphazard, friendly or downright dangerous! One cannot expect to be made welcome wherever one goes, especially if you are not buying. Some yards do not mind 'browsers'; others have suffered thefts, damage and annoyance and so tend to be particular precisely who they allow in.

As long as there have been trucks, we have had scrapyards: there were plenty of breakers yards in horsedrawn days. Naturally, the contents of the yards have changed with the passing of time. In 1950, there were yards containing cars, trucks and fire engines from the World War One period, but their stocks have turned over many times since then and today anything prewar is very rare.

Scrapyards act as a magnet to old vehicle enthusiasts, for they can be the source of interesting 'finds' of both complete vehicles or at least parts required for a restoration. The photograph above was taken in a small yard near the old A1 road north of London which contained a Jeffery Quad, AEC B-type bus and the Leyland Tigers and model AA Ford shown.

Nothing very rare at first glance in this Hertfordshire scrapyard, just a group of 1930s machines including AEC, Dennis, Sentinel, Garner, Morris and Albion, none of which survived the cutting torch. But then, that is part of the attraction of such places, for it is often the things which are not readily seen that could be just what are sought, be it a complete and restorable vehicle or just some parts.

What regrets truck enthusiasts have when reminded about vehicles which were available just a few years ago! This Leyland Octopus was only one of the dozens of interesting vehicles to be found in yards all over the country when the HCVC was in its infancy. But, of course, it all depends on just what each individual finds worthy of restoring.

Index

A.R. MARSHALL & SONS LTD
LAU